SING and PLAY
GROWING UP

Pie Corbett

Chrysalis Children's Books

JELLY ON A PLATE

Jelly on a plate.
Jelly on a plate.
Wibble, wobble,
Wibble wobble,
Jelly on a plate.

LYING DOWN

Baby lying down.
Baby lying down.
Gaze, gaze, gaze around,
Baby lying down.

Baby sitting up.
Baby sitting up.
Pat, pat, bang, crash,
Baby sitting up.

Baby crawling by.
Baby crawling by.
Here, there, everywhere,
Baby crawling by.

Baby toddling round.
Baby toddling round.
Waddle, waddle, thump bump!
Baby toddling round.

THINGS TO TALK ABOUT

Look at this baby.

What do you think babies need?

What did you do when you were a baby?

THINGS TO DO

Make a simple picture frame!

You need

photo of you
as a baby

piece of
card

glue

sequins

shiny
paper

glitter

1. Draw around
your photo so
that you have
a 'frame'
to decorate.

2. Glue on
sequins,
glitter
and shiny
paper.

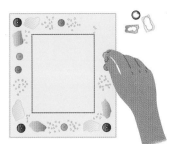

3. Stick your photo down in
the centre of the card.

4. Now you
have a lovely
picture frame
to keep in
your bedroom!

MOCKING BIRD

Hush little baby, don't say a word,
Papa's going to buy you a mocking bird.

And if that mocking bird won't sing,
Papa's going to buy you a diamond ring.

And if that diamond ring turns to brass,
Papa's going to get you a looking glass.

And if that looking glass gets broke,
Papa's going to get you a billy-goat.

And if that billy-goat gets away,
Papa's going to buy you another today.

JUST OUT OF BED

Just out of bed,
Splish, splash, splosh!
Brush your teeth
And have a wash.

Just before lunch,
You should be seen
Washing your hands
'Til they are clean.

Just after playing,
Now what to do?
Tidy up the mess
And say 'thank you'.

Just before bedtime,
Do you like a laugh?
Brush your teeth
And have a bath!

THINGS TO TALK ABOUT

Lets look at teeth.

Why do we have teeth?

When you bite an apple do you use the teeth at the front or the back?

Who do you visit to look after your teeth?

Think up 3 rules for keeping your teeth healthy.

8

THINGS TO DO

Make a hand print!

You need

saucer   paint   paper

1. Pour some paint into a saucer.

2. Put your hand into the paint, then press it on to some paper.

3. Try making a print every six months.

4. Ask an adult to make a hand print, too.

Are your hands growing?

Who has the largest print?

NOISE

Billy is blowing his trumpet;
Bertie is banging a tin.
Betty is crying for mummy
And Bob has pricked Ben with a pin.
Baby is crying out loudly;
He's out on the lawn in his pram.
I am the only one silent
And I've eaten half of the jam.

WHAT TEENAGERS DO

Sandy is dancing to disco,
Frankie is playing the drums.

Tasha is doing her make up,
And Alfie is tapping his thumbs.

Megan is doing her hair,
And Barry is going down town.

Jade is on the computer
And Jim is playing the clown.

Boris is out on his skateboard,
Timmy is phoning a friend.

Sally and Ally are chasing boys,
I'm wondering where it will end!

THINGS TO TALK ABOUT

Look at people's hair in
your class.

How many different hair colours can
you see?

How many different hairstyles
can you see?

Why do you think we have hair?

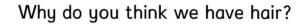

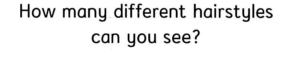

What do these people use to keep it
looking nice?

12

THINGS TO DO

Make a funny face pizza!

You need

 a pizza base

 slices of tomato

grated cheese

 black olives

 slices of green pepper

 slice of mushroom

1. Put the slices of tomato and grated cheese on to the pizza base.

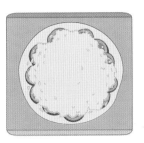

2. Add olives for eyes and green pepper for a mouth.

3. Add a slice of mushroom for a nose.

4. Ask an adult to bake the pizza for about 10 minutes at 180°C/350°F/ gas mark 4. Mmmmm!

THE MUMMIES ON THE BUS

The mummies on the bus go yakety-yak,
Yakety-yak, yakety-yak.
The mummies on the bus go yakety-yak,
All day long.

The children on the bus go chat, chat, chat,
Chat, chat, chat, chat, chat, chat.
The children on the bus go chat, chat, chat,
All day long.

The daddies on the bus fall fast asleep,
Fast asleep, fast asleep.
The daddies on the bus fall fast asleep,
All day long.

THE FAMILIES AT HOME

The families at home take tea together,
Tea together, tea together.
The families at home take tea together,
All afternoon.

The mummies at home will paint the room,
Paint the room, paint the room.
The mummies at home will paint the room,
All afternoon.

The daddies at home will rock the baby,
Rock the baby, rock the baby.
The daddies at home will rock the baby,
All afternoon.

The children at home play on the floor,
On the floor, on the floor.
The children at home play on the floor,
All afternoon.

THINGS TO TALK ABOUT

What do mummies and daddies
do while we are at school?

The nurse looks after
people who are ill.

The teacher helps children.

The bus driver takes
people to the shops.

The editor works at
the computer.

The firefighter puts out fires.

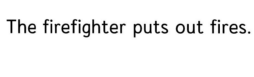

THINGS TO DO

Measure your height!

You need

ruler   pen or pencil

1. Find a place to measure yourself. (But make sure you ask an adult first!) Stand barefoot and upright against the wall.

2. Ask someone to lower a ruler gently on to your head and mark the wall with a pencil.

3. Measure yourself every six months. You will see that you are growing!

WHEN SUSIE WAS A BABY

When Susie was a baby,
a baby Susie was.
She went a gaa, gaa – gaa, gaa, gaa.

When Susie was a toddler,
a toddler Susie was.
She went a hi, hi – hi, hi, hi.

When Susie was a teenager,
a teenager Susie was.
She went a blar, blar – blar, blar, blar.

When Susie was a mummy,
a mummy Susie was.
She went a rock, rock – rockety rock.

When Susie was a granny,
a granny Susie was.
She went knit, knit – lost my stitch …

WHEN TOMMY WAS A GRANDPA

When Tommy was a grandpa, a grandpa Tommy was.
He read a book – look, look – I read my book!

When Tommy was a grandpa, a grandpa Tommy was.
He liked to sing – tra-la-la – I like to sing!

When Tommy was a grandpa, a grandpa Tommy was.
He liked to chatter – chitter chatter – I like to natter.

 When Sally was a grandma, a grandma Sally was.
She liked to sew – in, out – I like to sew.

When Sally was a grandma, a grandma Sally was.
She rocked the baby – there, there – rockety rock.

 When Sally was a grandma, a grandma Sally was.
She drove her car – brum, brum – I drive my car.

THINGS TO TALK ABOUT ?

Look at these people.

1. Who do you think is the youngest?

2. Who is the oldest?

3. Who is about your age?

4. Who could be a grandparent?

THINGS TO DO

Play the game 'Grandma's footsteps'.

One of you is chosen to be 'grandma'.

Grandma stands facing a wall.

Everyone else stands well back.

Then they creep towards grandma.

If she turns around, everyone freezes.

If she sees anyone wobbling then they must sit down.

The winner is the first person to touch grandma. Hurray!

RHYME ACTIONS

Why not add some actions to the rhymes to make them fun?
Here are a few to get you started but you could make up your own too!

marching

turning around

going to sleep

reaching high

waving side to side

flying a plane

rocking a baby

touching the floor

dancing

stepping
side to side

talking on
the phone

stretching wide

HOW THE BOOK WORKS

The book is divided into five units: babies, children, teenagers, mums and dads, and grandmas and grandpas. Each unit comprises 4 pages.

 The first page of each unit features a well-known nursery rhyme or traditional rhyme.

 On the second page of the unit the words to the rhyme have been changed so that children can sing about a topic, learning basic information in an enjoyable way.

 The third page of the unit provides a topic for discussion where children can draw on their own experience and broaden their knowledge.

 The fourth page offers an activity for children to get really involved.

TEACHERS' AND PARENTS' NOTES

Where you see an 'open book' icon in the bottom right corner of a page, this indicates that there are further ideas, suggestions or an explanation about the page's contents.

Page 4 Ask the children to bring in photo(s) of themselves when they were babies. How have they changed? What can they do now that they couldn't do as a baby? You could make a photo timeline of them from being a newborn to being a toddler. This provides an opportunity to discuss how we change as we grow.

Page 12 Ask the children to draw their face and make their own hairstyle by cutting lengths of wool in different colours. Display the faces and hairstyles and use them to talk about how we are all different.

Page 15 Ask the children to add to the verses of this rhyme to talk about what they and their family do at home.

Index

First published in the UK in 2005 by
Chrysalis Children's Books
An imprint of Chrysalis Books Group Plc,
The Chrysalis Building, Bramley Road,
London W10 6SP

ISBN 1 84458 332 5

British Library Cataloguing in Publication Data
for this book is available from the British Library.

Associate Publisher *Joyce Bentley*
Project Editor *Debbie Foy*
Editorial Assistant *Camilla Lloyd*
Designer *Paul Cherrill*
Illustrators *Ed Eaves, Jo Moore and Molly Sage*

Printed in China

10 9 8 7 6 5 4 3 2 1

Typography *Natascha Frensch*
Read Regular, READ SMALLCAPS and Read Space; European
Community Design Registration 2003 and Copyright ©
Natascha Frensch 2001-2004 Read Medium, **Read Black** and
Read Slanted Copyright © Natascha Frensch 2003-2004

READ™ is a revolutionary new typeface that will enhance
children's understanding through clear, easily recognisable
character shapes. With its evenly spaced and carefully
designed characters, READ™ will help children at all stages
to improve their literacy skills, and is ideal for young readers,
reluctant readers and especially children with dyslexia.